THE MOON WALKER

The Moon Walker

by Paul Showers

Illustrated by Susan Perl

Doubleday & Company, Inc.
Garden City, New York

Text Copyright © 1975 by Paul Showers
Illustrations Copyright © 1975 by Susan Perl
All Rights Reserved
Printed in the United States of America
First Edition

Library of Congress Cataloging in Publication Data

Showers, Paul.
    The moon walker.

    SUMMARY: Describes the physical development of an infant as he learns to use his hands, mouth, feet, and otherwise adjust to life in his new environment.
    1. Infants (Newborn)—Juvenile literature.
[1. Infants. 2. Growth] I. Perl, Susan, illus.
II. Title.
RJ251.S45   612.6'54
ISBN 0-385-01945-9 Trade
      0-385-02042-2 Prebound
Library of Congress Catalog Card Number 73-17490

We saw movies yesterday of men walking on the moon.

They wore big space suits and walked around in them.
It wasn't easy to walk.
They picked up their feet slowly.
They couldn't turn around very fast.
They looked funny when they tried to jump.

They were learning how to use their space suits.
They were learning how to walk in them—
        and run
                and jump.
You have to learn a lot of things when you land on the moon.

We have a moon walker in our family.
His name is Christopher. He is my baby brother.
He landed here on earth just a year ago.
That was the day he was born in the hospital.
We call it his birthday.

Mommy and Daddy brought him home the next week.

Christopher has been our moon walker ever since.
A baby has to learn a lot of things when he lands on the earth.
Christopher is learning how to use *his* space suit.
His space suit is his body.

He has to get used to every part of it—
    eyes
        mouth
            hands
                legs
                    feet.

He could do something else, too.
"Put your finger in his hand," Mommy said.
I did. Christopher held on tight to my finger.
"Little babies can't use their hands to pick up things," Mommy said.
"But they know how to hold on."

Christopher was tiny when he came home.
His eyes didn't open very wide.
He couldn't sit up. He didn't know how to talk.
He had to wear diapers.
"He doesn't know how to turn off the water," Daddy said.

Christopher could do three things—
    sleep
        eat

Christopher soon learned to use his eyes.
He opened them wide every day and looked at things.
One day he saw his hands. He seemed very interested.
He used his eyes to look at his hands for a long time.

He began to look at other things.
When I shook the rattle, he turned his head to look at it.
When I held up his rabbit, he looked at that.

At first Christopher didn't look at me when I said "Hello."
One day I was lying on the floor beside him.
I was talking to him.
He was looking all around and waving his feet.

I looked into his eyes.
I smiled and told Christopher I liked him.
He looked into my eyes.
I told him he was a fine baby brother.

Christopher didn't know what I was saying.
But when he looked in my eyes, he saw how I felt.
He knew I liked him.
He began to kick and wave his arms.
He made little sounds in his throat.
I think he wanted to say something to me.
"He doesn't know how to work his telephone," Daddy said.

Every day I talked to Christopher.
I told him all sorts of things—
    about school—about my friends—all sorts of things.
Christopher didn't know what I was saying,
    but he liked it when I talked to him.
One day he smiled at me.
After that he smiled every day.

Another day Mommy picked him up and Christopher laughed.
It wasn't a big laugh. It was just a short giggle.
But it got bigger every day.
Daddy would hold Christopher up high and let him down fast.
Christopher liked that. It always made him laugh.
Sometimes it made him hiccup, too.
"He's got his hiccups and his laughs mixed up," Daddy said.
"Some day he'll learn not to."

Soon Christopher found he could make sounds with his voice.
Every day he made more and more sounds.
He would lie on his back and kick and squeal.
He would look at his toys and say "Coooooo."
He made funny noises with his lips.
"He's beginning to learn to talk," Mommy said.

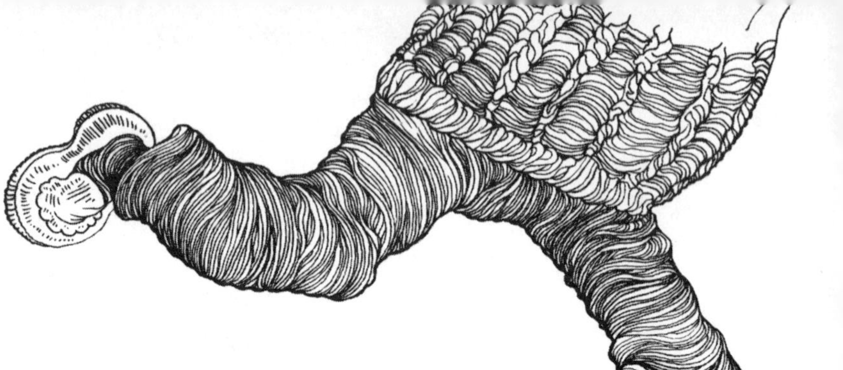

Christopher liked his bath.
He liked the water and would splash and kick.
He learned to sit up by himself in the water.
Then he learned to pick up the washrag and put it in his mouth.

He wanted to pick up the rubber duck, too.
At first he didn't know how.
He reached for the duck and waved his fingers.
The duck just floated away.
Christopher kept trying. One day he grabbed the duck
    and held on. He kept his fingers tight.
He put the duck in his mouth.
After that Christopher began to pick up all sorts of things—
    his rattle—his rabbit—his orange elephant.

Christopher learned to pick up tiny things, too.
He used his thumb and first finger.
He liked to pick up the crumbs on his plate and put them in his mouth.
When he was on the floor, he picked up little bits of paper—and dust.
He put them in his mouth, too.
"Oh dear!" Mommy said. "He's a regular vacuum cleaner."
"Never mind," Daddy said. "He's just learning how those hands work."

Christopher had to learn to eat and drink.
At first he could only suck on his bottle.
Then Mommy began to feed him with a spoon.
She fed him cereal and applesauce and mashed bananas.

Christopher liked these things, but he didn't know how to chew.
And his mouth got mixed up.
He forgot to swallow. Cereal spilled out of his mouth.
Daddy gave him orange juice in a cup, but Christopher didn't know how to hold his lips.
The orange juice ran down his chin.
Christopher was very messy.
"It takes time to find out how to do these things," Mommy said.
"Wait till he gets his teeth."

Christopher got his first teeth when he was about seven months old.
They were front teeth—two of them.
At first they made his mouth sore.
He was fussy and cried a lot.
Mommy gave him a rubber ring. He chewed it.
That made his mouth feel better.

When Christopher was tiny, he didn't move much.
He slept on his stomach.
But he grew bigger. And stronger.
He learned to raise his head and look around.

Christopher didn't want to lie on his stomach all the time.
He tried to turn over. It was hard.
He waved his arms. He kicked his feet.
He didn't get anywhere.

Soon he learned to push with one foot.
He turned on his side and pushed.
When he pushed hard enough, he flopped over on his back.
Every time Mommy put him down on his stomach, Christopher turned over on his back.
He did this for several days.

Then he tried to turn over on his stomach.
He kicked with his legs. He arched his back.
It was hard work. He made grunting sounds.
"Don't help him," Mommy said. "He wants to do it by himself."
Sometimes Christopher gave an angry yell.
"Listen to that," Daddy said. "I think he's swearing."
At last Christopher learned to turn over on his stomach.

After that he turned over and over every day.
Over on his back
                 over on his stomach
                                 on his back again.
He was learning to use his legs and arms and his body.

One day Christopher was on his stomach.
He tried to reach his elephant. It was too far away.
He tried to make his body move forward.
He waved his arms. He kicked.
Daddy watched him. "He'll take off one of these days," Daddy said.

Soon Christopher began to crawl.
First he learned to get up on his hands and knees.
He rocked back and forth.

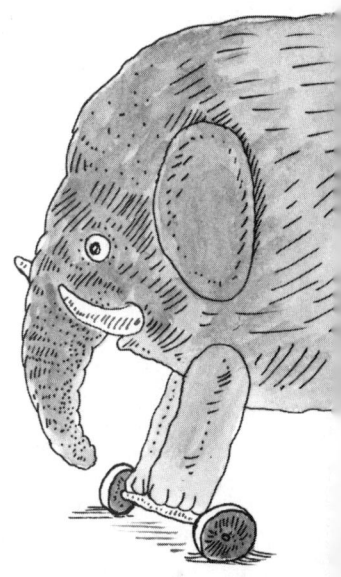

Sometimes he rocked too hard and fell over on his face.
But he kept working.
Little by little he learned how to move his hands and knees.
He stopped flopping on his face.
Once he learned how, he crawled everywhere.

Then he wanted to stand up.
He would crawl to a chair and grab the leg.
He would pull himself up and stand by the chair.
Christopher liked to do this but it scared him.
He didn't know how to get down again.
He was afraid to let go of the chair. Once he cried.
"Let him alone," Mommy said. "He'll learn."
He did. Christopher learned very soon.

He would stand every day.
Climb up beside the chair. Sit down.
Climb up beside the table. Sit down.
Over and over again.
He learned to use his legs and arms in different ways.

Last month Christopher tried something new.
He climbed up and stood by the chair.
He put out one foot.
He let go of the chair with his hands.
He tried to go over to the table standing up.
He lost his balance and fell down.

That didn't stop Christopher.
He tried it again. And again.
Every time he fell down, he got up again.
Soon he could take two or three steps without falling.
Today he can stagger clear across the room without falling.

"He's just getting started," Mommy says.
"Watch him. Every day he gets better.
"He'll learn to run and skip and turn somersaults.
"Soon he'll begin to say words and to talk to us."

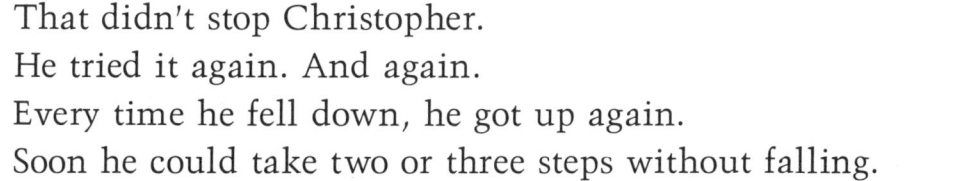

Christopher doesn't go to school yet.
But he is learning things every day.
He learns like the men walking on the moon.
It isn't easy, but it's fun. He never gives up.
Christopher is learning how to live on the earth.

PAUL SHOWERS is, among other things, a grandfather, a long-time newspaper man, and the author of over twenty books. He was graduated from the University of Michigan in 1931 and has been with both the New York *Herald Tribune* and the New York *Times,* the latter for the last twenty-seven years.

Born in Vienna, SUSAN PERL was kicked out of art school there for "lack of drawing ability." Nonetheless, she began drawing fashion illustrations for *Vogue* in her early teens, and has since illustrated several books and numerous articles in the *New York Times* and many magazines. Her disarming drawings of freckled kids and fluffy animals reveal Ms. Perl's love of artless creatures, her first and foremost preoccupation.